ESCAPE

ESCAPE

and other poems

by

Leslie Hodge

© 2024 Leslie Hodge. All rights reserved.
This material may not be reproduced in any form, published,
reprinted, recorded, performed, broadcast,
rewritten, or redistributed without
the explicit permission of Leslie Hodge.
All such actions are strictly prohibited by law.

Cover design by Shay Culligan

ISBN: 978-1-63980-654-6

Kelsay Books
502 South 1040 East, A-119
American Fork, Utah 84003
Kelsaybooks.com

for

Bill and Suzy

Acknowledgments

Thank you to the editors of the following publications where some of these poems first appeared.

Arkansas Review: "Summer"
Catamaran Literary Reader: "Green Flash"
In Parenthesis: "Escape"
The Journal of Undiscovered Poets: "Viking Queen"
The Main Street Rag: "Red," "The Woods at Twilight"
The Muleskinner Journal: "At the Cal Neva"
Pigeon Pages: "Velázquez at the Prado"
The Poeming Pigeon: "The Big Question"
The San Diego Union-Tribune: "We Smile with Our Eyes"
Sisyphus Lit Magazine: "Waiting on Your Wings to Dry"
Smoky Blue Literary and Arts Magazine: "Martha Stewart Living," "The Three-Dog Leash"
South Florida Poetry Journal: "Chicago Winter 1978–1979"
SPANK the CARP: "Christmas Tree"
Your Daily Poem: "Universal Donor," "The Cowboy, the Cook, and the Horse"

Contents

Red	11
Viking Queen	12
Waiting on Your Wings to Dry	14
Velázquez at the Prado	16
Chicago Winter 1978–1979	17
Martha Stewart Living	18
Love Me Still	19
Universal Donor	20
High Dive	21
At the Fair	22
Past the Rest Stop	24
We Smile with Our Eyes	25
The Cowboy, the Cook, and the Horse	27
The Big Question	29
Escape	31
Summer	32
Christmas Tree	34
Near Spring Creek Gap	36
At the Cal Neva	37
Raised on Country Music	40
The Three-Dog Leash	41
Green Flash	43
Paint-by-Number	44
Tomorrow	45
I Am Not a Cowgirl	46
The Woods at Twilight	49

Red

What is this thing? This *Riding Hood,*
and yet the girl does not ride.

There is no horse to lure the wolf,
only the girl, who carries the hatchet

hid in her basket. The weight worries
her wrist as she walks, quickly, with stealthy

backward glances, barely avoiding
the roots and the branches.

Where is the woodsman and his ax,
invented by the Brothers Grimm,

or men like them, to save her?
Red was tougher than she knew.

When the woodsman came at last,
he peered through the open window,

turned and ran away, the forest
closing like a door behind him.

Viking Queen

Whales sing for the Viking queen—
she's hard and cruel and cold.
Dual-headed dragon boat,
twenty oars as long as oaks,
pulled by forty weary men.
Eighty cracked and calloused hands
pull. And pull. And pull again.

The moon a scythe, shreds the clouds,
opens up a map of stars.
She tilts her face up, fox fur-fringed,
breathes in, tastes the wind,
and with a flutter of her fingers
signals to the oarsmen.

Her eyes green as glaciers breaking,
just as hard and cold.
The men no longer warm in bear skins,
ice forms on their braided beards.
They strain and suffer her command.
Yet with a single sideways glance,
they could easily drop the oars,
rise and throw her overboard.

They think that they would like to see her
in the glow of moon and starlight
as a speck of jetsam, bobbing,
while the chill of white-fringed waves
soaks her clothes, pulls her under.

And yet. She knows where whales swim.
Guides the boat past icebergs rising
higher than the painted sail.
Sees beyond the vast horizon,
steely ocean touching sky.

And so. Although she's cruel and cold,
she reads the stars. She knows the way.

Waiting on Your Wings to Dry

Sitting in a low beach chair, you time the sets, sea and sky
a celestial blue. You touch the switch to make your halo solid—
Renaissance style—and tilt it so your face is shaded.
Your long white robes are tossed on the sand by your
water-into-wine bottle. You're nearly naked but nobody notices.

Gulls land behind you squawking, eye your feathers with beady
eyes, turn their heads as if checking with each other—Us? Us? Us?
You rise and open your wings full size to shoo the birds away, then
   fold
them up and walk lightly into the water, shimmering with gold
   flecks.

Deeper you go until the waves knock you about.
You tuck your wings tight and dive under, sand and salt
in your nose, rising with one eye open to check the coming swells.

Above the waves' roar you hear yelling—a man and a woman
are running down the beach, shouting, "Jimmy! Jimmy! Jimmy!"

The next wave slams you under. You rise, feathers floating
in bubbles. Far away a boy on a boogie board is carried by a rip.

As if body surfing, you use the next wave to slingshot into
the sky, wings spread to catch the updraft. You bump a hang-glider,
breathe out to float him away, turn, fly fast following the rip
   current.

Scattering a string of pelicans, you dive for the boy—is he six?
   five?
Human ages are tough. He's small enough you can tuck his head
under your chin and murmur, "There, there.
Do you see the dolphins? Let's look for dolphins."

Sure enough, a pod surfaces and races with you, leaping
and laughing, toward the beach where the Mom and the Dad
are crying, surrounded by lifeguards clad, barely, in Baywatch red.

Closer to shore, kayakers wave their paddles and shout
  encouragement.
A standup paddleboarder staggers, and you steady him with a wing
  tip.

You descend gliding, wings spread, like Jesus appearing to the
  lifeguard apostles
who cheer as Mom and Dad take Jimmy and cover him with
  kisses.

But really, at this moment you feel more like the Botticelli Venus.

Modestly accepting their thanks, you archly open and close your
  wings a few times,
scattering saltwater droplets, then walk to your chair, shoo the
  gulls away.
Glancing back, you see Jimmy raise his small hand in benediction.
Turning to watch the waves, you eat your lunch—divinity and
  angel food cake.

Velázquez at the Prado

ode to the Rokeby Venus

Beyond the stanchioned velvet ropes,
an ivory backside tinged with pink.
Cupid clasps a cloudy mirror
for Venus.

                                        Mortals pause,
                                     enthralled by her
                             velvety voluptuousness.

Travel-weary, we vault over the ropes
and melt into the painting's oil,
ignoring the cries of the
outraged guards.

                                    We say to Venus
                         Move over, dear, casting off
clothes smelling faintly of turpentine.

Gratefully, we recline. Venus smiles.
Cupid turns, angles the mirror
so that the guards can see

                                    themselves, with
                   brush-stroked open mouths,
           wondering   what   just happened.

We drift off and dream of Velázquez
in Italy on a working vacation.
Idly he mixes the color
of fantasy-flesh.

                                          He's thinking,
                                    Come and get me,
                          Copper! or whatever is

the era-appropriate expression
of the baroque Spanish Inquisition.

Chicago Winter 1978–1979

They were gloves of grey cashmere
that I could not afford to lose—

wonderfully warm and soft
when the wind howled off the lake,

and sleeting snow profiled the face
of the fifty-foot Picasso

dominating Daley Plaza.
Plodding toward the Lake Street El,

head down, I stumble off the curb
into the frozen slush. My shoes

are soaked and cold. A taxi drifts
toward me, yellow in the gray.

Cabs were cheap then. Warm inside,
gloves on my lap, we're driving north

on Lake Shore Drive. The cabbie looks
like my dad. *"Ah, you're going*

to break some hearts," he says, taking
the fare, then pulling away while I

stand in the swirl of snow, knee deep
and rising—cold, and gloveless again.

Martha Stewart Living

Arriving late at Turkey Hill,
milky moon, no snow yet.
Inside the house are candles set
at each windowsill.

What shall I do this fortnight?
Picking up an antique quill,
I dip it in the inkwell
and write by candlelight.

Shear the shy alpacas; spin and dye the yarn.
Rake and dry the maple leaves. Save for the Bonfire.
Embroider scenes of Mt. Fuji, cross-stitch and French knots.
Butcher poor old Wilbur—such an unfortunate name.
    Start the hams in the smokehouse, make sausage with wild sage.
Oil the treadle sewing machine, stitch masks from old linen.
Gather chicken and turkey eggs, save the shells for gilding.
Bake dog treats for Genghis Khan. Ask him, who's a good boy?
Don the gold kimono; write haiku and tanka.
Curry the Shetland ponies. Curl and color the manes.
Make the giant marshmallows; heat the hand-pressed cider.
    Invite Cook and Maid and Gardener to the last Bonfire.

The magazine slips off the bed,
life luxurious and sweet.
I pull the Martha Stewart sheets
up over my head.

Love Me Still

after W. B. Yeats, "For Anne Gregory"

Retirement is here now.
Therefore, my only care
is how to spend my time
in weather foul or fair.
Those who love me, love me still
despite my snow-white hair.

Career clothes are abandoned.
Gone, my fashion flare.
Long and loose my look now—
I don't care what I wear.
Those who love me, love me still
and like my cloud-white hair.

My face lined like a roadmap
greets me in the mirror.
No make-up masks my face now.
I'll put no color there.
Those who love me, love me still
and love my pearl-white hair.

Universal Donor

Wasn't I proud
to walk into the Blood Bank
wearing my 4-gallon pin?

And didn't I carefully
check off the boxes,
pass the iron and
blood pressure tests?

And wasn't I *noble,* lying
down on the chair, a slick stiff
recliner, so willing to give
the *O-positive* essence
of myself?

And wasn't it brave of me,
so the nurse said, repeatedly
digging into my elbow
with what—a crochet hook?

And weren't we all jolly,
with our orange juice and Oreos,
hooked to machines and tubes,
saving lives?

And was I not piqued then, was I not
vexed, when the nurse
in holiday scrubs let slip

the Universal Donor
is *O-negative?*

High Dive

Your toes grip the grit of the board
as you flex your knees and bite your lip,
weighing how much mocking you could endure
if you climbed down the ladder to the pool deck.

Chlorine rises, sharp, in your nose,
the sun is burning the tops of your ears.
The water shows its teeth and lures you.
Girlfriends splashing, laughing, yelling,

    Come on!

        The water's great!!

            Jump in!!!

From the bottom of the pool
you see their legs and feet, swirling,
while you hold your breath and count
all the ways you hate them.

At the Fair

If you go to the fair, you will be changed.
The roller-coaster terrifies, and there
will be a creepy funhouse feeling. Wheel
of fortune spins. Bagged goldfish prize for first
place won't survive—they are not worth the money
lavished by the suckers at the fair.

Huge turkey legs are gnawed on at the fair.
At Chicken Charlie's, food's profoundly changed.
Your eyes conspire to cast away your money
for culinary combinations there—
hamburgers bunned in Krispy Kremes? But first,
a blooming onion bigger than a wheel.

Many baby buggies, bikes, and wheel-
chairs make it tough to navigate the fair.
Distressed toddlers scream and cry at first—
those babies then contented, fed and changed,
kick their feet and coo. You can see there,
their families love them more than food or money.

Take out a bank loan, just to get the money
you'll need to park and enter. Grab the wheel
of your life and drive fast to get there—
the midway, San Diego County Fair.
At booths where cards are charged and bills are changed,
which rides or food or junk will you buy first?

Elbow your way through crowds so you'll be first
to ride the Tilt-a-Whirl. Squander your money
for chances to win prizes. Feel short-changed
when you spin the Lotto spinning wheel.
Hey! Nobody said that life was fair!
Enjoy the livestock and woodworking there.

We spent our money to go to the fair.
We were the first ones on the Ferris wheel.
And changed and broke we were, when we left there.

Past the Rest Stop

Hard journey, sailing west
to east, the schooner scraping
old asphalt of Route 66.

When the wind dies, we drop
the sails and nose-in to dock by
a teepee motel.
     VACANCY

Sunset streaks the sky more
colors than a neon Navajo
blanket. Night wind rocks
the boat, rattlesnake coils
the keel. We sleep fitfully, apart.

In the morning children
emerge, peek
into portholes. Morning
chill makes their breath
     balloons
for cartoon dialogue.

Their eyes don't blink,
watching as we struggle with the sail.
Where are you from? a child asks,
     Where are you going?

We Smile with Our Eyes

March 2020

We smile with our eyes now
above the masks
made from bandanas and scarves.

Words are muffled, glasses fog.
Are we now desperados?
Harem dancers?
No matter, no matter—
we wave, tilt our heads,
all is new, all is novel.

How far is six feet?
Everyone knows now:
a double arms-length,
radius of
the sphere of safety (maybe).
Stay away, step aside.

Yellow police tape,
torn and tattered,
circles the playgrounds,
blocks parking lots.
Duck under, step over,
or break through the tape—
Or stop. Show yourself.
Just stop.

Invisible killer.
Silent assassin.
Moves in a mist
too fine to feel.
Overruns your defenses,
burns your blood,
floods your lungs.

Anti-social distance
keeps us alive now,
so we pray, so we hope.
And yet we smile.
We smile with our eyes.

The Cowboy, the Cook, and the Horse

He raises both hands
and tips back his hat—
a round, sweat-stained halo
that circles his head—
and his elbows thus raised
look like angel wings
although of the sharp
and pointy shape.
He busts out his chest
'til his buttons, they snap
open, revealing
the red underwear
favored by cowboys
at home on the range.
Then he flings his leg over
the pommel and leaps
off like a trout
with an eye on the fly,
lands hard on his heels,
his spurs all a-jingle,
and walks in a cloud
of dust raised from his chaps,
while his eyes roam the ridge
where the buffalo roam.
Now his horse can be hateful,
and given to biting
and bucking him off
on no provocation.
But he loves her and gives her
sugar and apples
he begs and he barters
for with the cook,

who seldom would speak
a discouraging word.
Cookie never lets on
he's happy to help him—
for what good is a cowboy
without a good horse?

The Big Question

after Ron Salisbury

I push the plate of avocado slices and lime wedges
toward Him, and the shaker of cayenne.
For a moment, His hands are busy. A contented sigh.
He touches the long wood table.

*My Son would like this. He knows something
about wood. Seats twelve?*

Thirteen. If you squeeze a little.
He looks down at the empty plate.
Oh, sorry. The other avocados are hard as rocks.
He shrugs, not wanting me to feel bad.

I could ripen them up?
I'm flustered. Oh! Wouldn't that be cheating?
He half-smiles while I think, what a dope!

So what was it you wanted to ask me?
Well, it's about Billy Collins. *Billy Collins?*
He smiles wider.

You gotta love a man who goes by Billy.

Yes. Yes, but here's the thing. What's with the Buddha?
The Buddha? Nice guy. He looks at me quizzically.

I mean, in the poems. You know, the one about shoveling
snow over his shoulder like a mountain. And the one
where the Buddha gets off the dashboard and starts walking.
You know.

Chuckling, He lays His hand on mine.
In His glittering eyes, galaxies collide.

Honestly, I have no idea.

Escape

Open the door to let the dog out,
a hummingbird flies in too fast to see,
then the *tap-tap-tap-tap* of a needle beak
on the inside of the window, the whir of wings.

I gasp, snap the dish towel and drop
a porcelain teacup—it shatters.

> *No hummingbird has made it inside before,*
> *although there have been a few other birds.*
> *And a lizard. Wasps and bees, naturally.*
> *Once a rattlesnake who sulked*
> *under the bookcase until animal control*
> *arrived with their loop on the long stick*
> *and a big burlap bag—bored and businesslike.*

Collapsed on the windowsill
palm-sized ruby-throated.
So still, I think he has died,
toothpick bones broken—
but no, he flurries and smashes
himself against the glass again.

Fast and frantic, I wrench open the window,
tear off the screen—and he escapes.

> *I know that longing,*
>   *to be among the birds-of-paradise.*

Summer

In the Ozark foothills, central Missouri,
a river called the Gasconade
flows south to north through woods and farmland—
feed corn, cattle, wild ponies, hay.

In winter, it floods. When my grandpa died,
the river rose in driving rain.
The tourist cabins at Indian Ford
were swept off their foundations, floated away.

Spring blooms the dogwood and redbud trees
that lean over the river, gravel-bottom and clear.
The towns are small, most folks are related.
You can't get away with anything.

Summers, the relatives gather and drive
to the river's edge, setting up under
the ironwork bridge. On lawn chairs arranged
around a stick fire, their talk meanders

much like the calf who trotted through town
past the WPA courthouse and Catholic church,
crossed the highway, toured the cemetery,
and kept on going. The women lean back

in chairs as they listen, lolled on one hip
and the opposite elbow, occasionally making
a snort of derision while the men tip back Pabst,
light cigarettes. The kids are swinging

from ropes tied to cottonwoods into the river,
splashing and swimming. Marshmallows on whittled
sticks set afire raise blisters and burns.
Ticks, chiggers, mosquitos are biting,

lightning bugs shine in palms and glass jars.
The river ripples, catches the moon
that silvers the trees. The last of the ice chest
is poured on the fire, chairs and blankets

are tossed into trunks and pickup trucks.
Good night. Good night. Goodbye. Good night.
After folks leave, the riverbank's quiet.
Head above water, a cottonmouth swims

by a necklace of catfish strung on a trotline.
Deer kneel down, velvet nose and ears twitching.
Do they dream of the shotguns and rifles of fall?
What is it to me that these memories linger?

I'm older now than any of them,
those cousins and grannies who laughed and argued
as mist rose and rolled like smoke on the river.
Good night. Good night. Goodbye. Good night.

Christmas Tree

The school bus doors fold open before a girl,
maybe eight, standing on the cattle grate.
At her feet a cedar lies, long as she is tall.

The air is cold glass holding back the heavy
snow that will be swirling once the sun
breaks through and the wind picks up.

Early this morning, she and her mother left the babies
fussing in the crib and set out with the hatchet
toward the stand of cedars, a half-mile from the house.

Now she stands before the school bus door.
The kids have moved to the side where the bus leans
toward the bar ditch, their breath clouding windows.

The driver is not mean, but he is strict. He is the
girl's grandfather. She can tell he does not want
that fresh-cut wet and sappy tree dragged into his bus.

Her round chin, like his, rises. "It's for school," she says.
"I told 'em I'd bring a tree." His eyes, brown like hers,
narrow. "For school?" A sigh. "Well. All right, then."

Turning his head over his shoulder, he says,
"You kids. Listen up. No more trees. If they ask you
to bring a tree to school, you tell 'em I said no."

The children laugh behind their mittened hands.
The scent of cedar spreads. They reach out, stroking
the branches as the girl drags her tree down the aisle.

The doors close and the engine strains. On the other
side of the gravel road, up a hill, a stand of trees
are outlined, white snow on black branches.

Come Eastertime, those dogwoods will release clouds
of snowy blossoms, massing ankle-deep on the ground.
Do not think of taking one of those trees on the school bus.

Near Spring Creek Gap

When I was barely a teenager my grandfather took me to the farm where he was born, The Old Home Place—a log cabin with a stone chimney, falling-down fences, and a barn. *The boys slept in the barn, in the loft,* Grandpa said. *With the horses and cows. Nice and warm.* It was springtime, but cool enough for coats. A blanket of daffodils, planted by Grandpa's mother, spread brilliant yellow, twenty feet out from the porch. The cabin was falling, fading, disintegrating, but we went inside. Old newspaper lined the walls, frayed and peeling. Upstairs was a bed with a rope and cornhusk mattress, and mouse droppings underneath. Pinned to the wall was a valentine showing an Eskimo girl by an igloo, under an arctic sun—inside, *To Momma, Love Anna.*

> Light drizzle spangles
> the worn outdoor furniture.
> I am warm inside.

At the Cal Neva

Stan rambles through the casino, no clocks, oxygen pumped in.
  Finally a two-dollar table.
Insurance? asks the dealer. Stan peeks at his hole card, smiles,
  waves his hand low.

His daughter Layla at the craps table shooting dice, her chips
  sorted by color.
The stickman sings out, too tall to call! He winks, nudging new
  dice to her.

Coming out! All the hard ways, working. The stickman raises one
  eyebrow.
Layla rolls a four, twenty-two, Little Joe. Says, place six. Place
  eight. Odds.

In the bar, her sisters Kiki and Joy swing onto the dance floor with
  sure-footed cowboys.
The tip jar by the singer's boot is overflowing. *Dim lights, thick
  smoke, and loud, loud music . . .*

What kind of beer do you have? Oh, says the waitress, you're
  asking the wrong person.
She swivels through the tables setting down shots and margaritas,
  idly eavesdropping—

*That girl singer, she ain't got a country voice. Yeah? Yeah,
  now look at Loretta.*
*She can rhyme hard and tired. You know, tard. Coal Miner's
  Daughter. Yeah?*

*This place is a dump. I wanna take one of those buses into Reno.
I'll take you, Ma.
What? I'll drive you to Reno. If I wanted a drunk to drive me, I'd
drive myself.*

*Hey, why don't you all come out to West End Beach tomorrow?
Where's that?
Donner Lake. Hmm, I think we're gonna go rafting on the Truckee.
Oh. Okay.*

At the table, the boxman raises his chin toward Layla. You've got good bone structure.
While his hands casually change chips, his eyes shift to Joy. Joy smiles. Not you.

She's still rolling? says Kiki. Yeah, at least a half hour, maybe more. The table's crowded.
Shouts surge louder with each throw. They brought in more chips for the bank. Twice.

Joy sniffs the tobacco stink on her sleeve. Gonna burn these when I get home.
Ask for a Heineken. Better than those cheap watery drinks. *Baby needs new shoes.*

Finally Layla craps out. She pushes her chips to the boxman, tosses tokes to the dealers.
They nod, tap the chip on the table. The pit boss says have a good night, ladies.

Cooling down with a longneck, Layla sits with Stan in the bar. The band's on break.
A young man drifts toward them, tentative, polite. Are you going to shoot again?

Kiki and Joy enter laughing, stepping over the line separating Nevada and California.
Through the open window flows the scent of sugar pines. No, Layla says. This is enough.

Raised on Country Music

In this old black and white photograph, his legs are crossed to balance a guitar. From his hands, though, you can tell he doesn't really know how to play. All the same, the smile and eyes are soft and open. He is pleased with himself. In this next picture, you see *Jimmy Hodge and the Ozark Wranglers,* the band in demand for pie suppers. He stands in the middle, hands clasped, eyes dreamy. Flanking him are two must-be-brothers with guitars. A tall young man raises a fiddle. Every one of them looks serious. They rode in his Model A to Rolla, to play on live radio. The brothers and their guitars were crammed into the rumble seat for 25 miles of snaky road. Here's the last picture. He's standing before a microphone, hands in his pockets, head tilted back, mouth open. On the old scratchy records they made, you can barely make out the words to *Frankie and Johnny.* They learned songs by listening to the Grand Ole Opry, the music in the voices making the words rhyme. Dad knew each and every Hank Williams song, and when he sang, I swear he sounded just like Ernest Tubb.

The Three-Dog Leash

1981

It seemed like a good idea. Three
mini dachshunds, short hair black-and-tan.
Low to the ground tripping hazard
tangling a handful of leashes to the handles.

"Here's your Christmas present, boys,"
said Dad, holding up the single leash
that split into three snap-hooks at the bottom.
The hot dogs barked and jumped vertical.

Gork, patrician, with AKC papers,
named for the famous racing greyhound Gork Lindsay.
Younger adopted brothers Zach and Cy, ruffians—no papers.
At first glance the tumbling wiener dogs are identical, except
for the colors of their collars: red, yellow, black.

Dad snapped on the three hooks—
instant dog-fight-on-a-leash.

2016

"Do not," my sister said,
"Put the dogs in with Mom and Dad."
Okay I said, thinking *What difference does it make?*
Then, *They'd be glad to have them along.*

2017

The pilot and the assistant pour
ashes into their containers,
breaking open the dogs' urns.

The runway rises to the west.
The plane turns, flying south along the coast. Near
the Del Mar racetrack, a smoke-gray plume
floats toward the blue water, followed a minute later
by a smaller plume.

2020

I hold the collars, jingling with tags.
Red for Gork E. Baba.
Yellow, Mr. Cy.
And Zachy-Boy? Well. Zach is black.

Green Flash

Here's where we saw it, Mom said
as she gestured with the arm
that wasn't leaning on mine.

We were walking slowly on the path
by the lake. Peeking through the pines
was a small blue triangle.
She looked at me expectantly.

> We had seen the green flash years ago,
> several times, on the beaches at Del Mar
> and Torrey Pines—brighter than a traffic light,
> swallowed by the Pacific in a mere second.

I opened my mouth to say, No,
not here, we didn't see
the green flash here.
But I couldn't.

> Sun, sea and physics make a minor miracle.
> How do you tally the bounty of blessings
> you did nothing to deserve—
> they rain on you without number.

The wind brushed back a thin curtain of boughs.
Mom said, *Right here,* and paused us.
Remember? Right here.

> I haven't seen a green flash since.
> I think I am unworthy.

Paint-by-Number

My daughter sent me a paint-by-number set. So now, when the afternoon sun streams in, I take up the thin brush. The set is called Greek Doors. There's lots of floral vegetation, a mosaic of very small shapes bearing numbers. These colors are called 1, 2, 3, 4, 5, 6, 7, 8 and 9. It's hard to keep color 5, a brilliant deep pink, within the lines. I find myself at the kitchen sink, washing out the brushes, getting ready to paint over my mistakes.

Tomorrow

for Bill

I have pearls from Hyderabad,
and from the Ponte Vecchio
golden rings, chains and charms.
Sterling silver, Mexico.

Emerald earrings from Brazil.
Strands of glass beads from Murano,
Ceylon sapphire, marquise-cut.
Old-pawn earrings, Navajo.

All this would I give and more—
jewels and gems, the mementos
of our travels, lives, and love—
for a thousand more tomorrows.

I'd buy or sell, lend or borrow
for, with you, one more tomorrow.

I Am Not a Cowgirl

I am not a cowgirl
Though I covet gloves with fringe.
I'd saw the reins and flick the hoss,
While riding on the ringe.

I am not a cowgirl,
Ain't got no Tony Lamas.
My mama took advice that Willie
Gave to cowboy mamas.

I am not a cowgirl.
Spurs just make me trip.
Riding along, the saddle horn
I hold in a death grip.

I am not a cowgirl,
Wearing chaps gives me a rash.
Chuck wagon food is not so good—
Those biscuits, beans and hash.

I am not a cowgirl,
Can't roll a cigarette.
While singing round the campfire,
There are words that I forget.

I am not a cowgirl.
I cannot yip and yo-del.
My idea of roughing it
Is staying in a mo-tel.

I am not a cowgirl,
I cannot rope nor ride.
My horse will snort as a retort,
His attitude is snide.

I am not a cowgirl.
Cold beers I do not try,
And when I order Chardonnay,
Bartenders roll their eyes.

I am not a cowgirl.
I have no bona fides.
No gun to shoot to get the loot,
No sidearm by my side.

I am not a cowgirl,
But my mama milked the cows
Be-fore school and after,
In the barn behind the howse.

I am not a cowgirl,
But my grandpa had Charolais.
He'd herd 'em in a pickup truck
And toss 'em bales of hay.

My uncle'd cut the yearlings
And he'd throw 'em in the dirt,
Notch their ears and brand 'em,
And cut 'em where it hurts.

I have a mini dachshund.
Her name is Audrey Dog.
It's "Get a looong little doggie,"
When it's time for her to jog.

Our daughter's name is Suzy girl.
We often joke and tease her,
Because although we love her so,
She's not a cowgirl neither.

My husband Bill's my pardner.
Being married's such a joy.
He came to Elko willingly,
Though he is no cowboy!

I am not a cowgirl,
But I am glad we met.
It might be rude to call me dude—
But you can call me—dudette.

Yodel-ay-ee-oh! Ay-ee-oh! Ay-ee!

The Woods at Twilight

If age is a notch slashed into a tree on a path
through overgrown forest, then death is the cliff at trail's end.
Grieving's a cloudburst hammering granite, and solace
the wavering rainbow. Memories, mouse skulls coughed up
by owls. The snake writes your name in the dust, sheds
his skin of bright promise. We are learning to read
the signs on the trail, feeling our way as the light fails.

Notes

The cover of this book features a photo of my maternal grandfather, T.C. Parker, from about 1930.

"Christmas Tree" is based on a true story as told to me by my mother, Sue Hodge, then called Oma Sue Parker.

"Raised on Country Music" was inspired by old photos of my father, James Leslie Hodge, when he sang on live radio.

I wrote "I Am Not a Cowgirl," the poem that started it all, to read at an open mic at The National Cowboy Poetry Gathering in Elko, Nevada, in January 2019.

Special thanks to Ron Salisbury for his great kindness and encouragement; to James Toupin for his close reading and generous critique; and to Ron Lauderbach for being my inspiration and guide.

Thanks also to the UCSD Osher Writers Workshop, including Janice Alper, Lucy Lehman, Elaine Olds, Angela Vasandani, Kamesh Gupta, and Rick Stein.

Special thanks to the outstanding poets, teachers and editors I've encountered: Michael Mark, Alison Luterman, Valentina Gnup, Rebecca Foust, Julia B. Levine, Taylor Byas, Katie Manning, Scott Douglass, Jayne Jaudon Ferrer, Catherine Segurson, Ken Schweda, and Tim Green.

Heartfelt appreciation for the members of The Poetry Salon, including Ron Lauderbach, Tammy Greenwood, Pat Obuchowski, Margaret Sullivan, Jen Laffler, Barb Thomson, June Chocoles, and Jennifer Karp. They keep me honest!

And most important, thank you to my husband Bill, our dear daughter Suzy, and my siblings, Kim, Jan, and Frank, for their steadfast encouragement and support.

About the Author

Leslie Hodge lives in San Diego with her husband Bill and mini-dachshund, Audrey Dog. After retiring, she studied with San Diego's first Poet Laureate, Ron Salisbury, and co-founded The Poetry Salon. Leslie writes poems to try to make sense of her life in a way that resonates with others.

Leslie's website is:
www.lesliehodgepoet.com

www.ingramcontent.com/pod-product-compliance
Lightning Source LLC
Chambersburg PA
CBHW030916170426

43193CB00009BA/877